Moral Reform Union.

THIRTEENTH ANNUAL REPORT.

1894-5.

To be obtained at the Office:

2, LEINSTER PLACE,
PORCHESTER TERRACE, LONDON, W.

PRICE SIXPENCE.

The Moral Reform Union.

ESTABLISHED IN THE INTERESTS OF PURE FAMILY LIFE.

Office:

2, LEINSTER PLACE, PORCHESTER TERRACE, LONDON, W.

Office Hours, 2.30—5.30 *p.m.*

MOTTO:—"*Thou shalt love thy neighbour as thyself.*"—Matt. xix. 19.

OBJECTS.

I. To study, and confer upon, all subjects which especially affect the moral welfare of the young.

II. To collect, sell, distribute, or publish Literature for Moral Education.

III. To consider how best to carry out practical measures for the reform of public opinion, law, and custom on questions of sexual morality.

THIS Union will be in communication with Societies engaged in any branch of the work, such as—

The Social Purity Alliance.
The Societies for the Abolition of State Regulation of Vice.
The Society for the Suppression of the Traffic in Girls.
The Societies for the Protection of Young Servants.
Young Men's Christian Association.
The Anti-Gambling League.
The Peace and Arbitration Associations.
The Vigilance Associations.
The Personal Rights Association,
and many others.

Reports and important papers of such Societies will be kept on hand.

No person eligible for *full* membership under the age of twenty-five.

The co-operation of members is invited for any branch of this work; and the business of the Union will continue to be conducted by those members who attend the meetings.

A Monthly Meeting is held at the Office on the first Wednesday of each month, and Ordinary Meetings on intermediate Wednesdays, at 3 p.m.

Drawing-room Meetings will be held occasionally, of which due notice will be given.

Subscriptions and Donations of any amount will be gladly received by

Hon. Treasurer,
Hon. Secretary, } 2, Leinster Place, W.
Miss F. E. ALBERT, *Secretary,* from 1881,

Bankers—THE NATIONAL BANK, 68, Gloucester Gardens, W.

The Moral Reform Union.

ESTABLISHED IN THE INTERESTS OF PURE FAMILY LIFE.

Office:

2, LEINSTER PLACE, PORCHESTER TERRACE, LONDON, W.

Office Hours, 2.30—5.30 p.m.

MOTTO:—"*Thou shalt love thy neighbour as thyself.*"—Matt. xix. 19.

OBJECTS.

I. To study, and confer upon, all subjects which especially affect the moral welfare of the young.

II. To collect, sell, distribute, or publish Literature for Moral Education.

III. To consider how best to carry out practical measures for the reform of public opinion, law, and custom on questions of sexual morality.

THIS Union will be in communication with Societies engaged in any branch of the work, such as—

The Social Purity Alliance.
The Societies for the Abolition of State Regulation of Vice.
The Society for the Suppression of the Traffic in Girls.
The Societies for the Protection of Young Servants.
Young Men's Christian Association.
The Gospel Purity Association.
The Peace and Arbitration Associations.
The Vigilance Associations,
and many others.

Reports and important papers of such Societies will be kept on hand.

No person eligible for *full* membership under the age of twe[nty-]five.

The co-operation of members is invited for any branch of [thi]s work; and the business of the Union will continue to be condu[cte]d by those members who attend the meetings.

A Monthly Meeting is held at the Office on the first Wednes[day] of each month, at 2.30 p.m., and Ordinary Meetings on interme[diate] Wednesdays, at 3 p.m.

Drawing-room Meetings will be held occasionally, of which notice will be given.

Subscriptions and Donations of any amount will be gladly receive[d]

Mrs. MIERS, *Hon. Treasurer*, 74, Addison Road, Kensington,

Mrs. S. W. BROWNE, *Hon. Sec.*, 58, Porchester Terrace, W.

Miss F. E. ALBERT, *Secretary.*

Bankers—THE NATIONAL BANK, 68, Gloucester Gardens, W.

MORAL REFORM UNION.

THIRTEENTH ANNUAL REPORT,

1894-95.

Outcome of last Annual Meeting :—

(I).—A Manifesto was issued, drawn up almost in the words of last year's Resolution, declaring that "in view of the serious danger to the honour and liberty of women involved (in all such practices as the C.D. and Indian Cantonments Acts) the signatories will not be satisfied until they have been made penal in every part of the world subject to the British Legislature."

This was widely circluated, at the cost of Miss Taylor (Hon. Secretary), to all Purity Societies and others. It received the names of many friends of Repeal at the Federation Conference in July, including that of Mrs. Butler. Several Chairmen of Associations and Officers signed for their Societies, this being notably so in the various branches of the Women's Christian Temperance Union of Canada, whom we have to thank for their support.

(II).—Another outcome was, Mrs. Woolcott Browne's hearty appreciation of Miss Taylor's speech, shewn by her presenting the Union with 1,000 copies of a reprint in leaflet form. This was circulated after the Meeting which welcomed Mr. A. S. Dyer, on his return from prison in India.

(III).—The vote of condolence with Mrs. Wm. Coote, widow of the late Honorary Secretary of the Social Purity Alliance, took the form of a framed Address. It expressed our grief that his disinterested labours should have shortened a life of such great promise—a brave and noble life—given with so much generosity to the great cause of human purity and happiness, and our confidence that his influence would live on in the hearts of the many whom his example has stimulated to work for Social Purity.

S.P.A.—We were glad to learn that the Secretaryship was filled by Mr. Eric Hammond (our Member since 1884) resuming the post he formerly held.

The S.P.A. this year sent us an order for single specimens of almost all the works on our white list.

Deputation to Sir Henry Loch, Governor of Cape Colony, on May 11th, 1894.—The M.R.U. being invited to send a delegate, Miss F. E. Albert, Secretary, attended, and read an Address. A selection of works was presented at the same time. By the generosity of Miss Taylor, the Address was printed, and some hundreds were distributed in Cape Colony; it was also sent to friends in India, Natal, Orange Free State, and Hobart.

Conferences.—At the 17th International Conference of the Federation for the Abolition of State Regulation of Vice, held in London, July 10th to 14th, seven delegates from the M.R.U. attended, and the Union's Manifesto and literature were distributed. *The Dawn*, for August, 1894, contains a report of that Conference.

To the Glasgow Conference of Women Workers, of October, 1894, we sent literature, the larger proportion of which was added by Miss Taylor.

We assisted the Meeting at Exeter Hall, in October, to welcome home from India Mr. Dyer and his fellow-sufferers, for whom we shared the unbounded sympathy expressed and shown by the Christian public of England.

Federation Work.—We gladly gave M. Minod addresses of correspondents abroad and at home, who might furnish information needed for a Congress, which is to be held this Summer in Paris, on Prisons and Penitentiaries. We also requested our Member, Miss Balgarnie, kindly to present to M. Minod her pamphlet on Police Matrons in Prisons.

India.—Important Social reforms have been continuously watched by us as both Bombay and Madras newspapers, edited by Native gentlemen, reach the Office by every mail; the encouraging feature of which attempts is, that the several reforms are being contended for by the enlightened aspirations of certain sections of the Native community.

We cannot omit to note the hopefulness springing from the succeding sessions of the Indian National Congress (apart from all political bearing), and notably, the stand that was made in the last Congress for the personal purity of public men.

Correspondence in Periodicals.—Extracts from *The Indian Spectator* of Oct. 7th, 1894, which repudiates Sir George White's views in favour of the C.D. Acts, were sent to Dr. Kate Bushnell, *The Dawn*, *The Sentinel*, *Personal Rights*, *the Woman's Signal*, and many other papers.

Traffic in Women.—We sent a letter to the *Indian Spectator*, pointing out the responsibility of Captains of ships in this matter.

Ceylon.—An order was sent us to supply a selection of works suitable for the Native Christians.

Burmah.—We read with gratitude Sir A. Mackenzie's speech at Mandalay last December, reproving those Government Officers who feign to take native wives, and abandon them because the union is not legally binding by English law.

Australia.—Miss Rosenhain, on returning to Australia, kindly took charge of a considerable quantity of literature for free distribution there.

Natal.—One of our most devoted members has taken up Mission Nursing in this Colony.

Japan and Philadelphia.—"The League of Justice" was sent to both these centres.

The Historical Library of the American Y.M.C.A. of Springfield, Mass., U.S.A., having asked us for a series of our reports and a selection of our literature, Miss Taylor generously undertook to have two volumes specially bound, and dedicated to the Historical Library.

Cleveland, Ohio, U.S.A.—Early in the year we were asked by Mr. J. W. Walton, a valued correspondent in Cleveland, to supply the Report of the Select Committee of the House of Lords of 1881, on the Protection of Girls, and also the Parliamentary Report of the same year on the C.D. Acts. These we were able to supply.

In the printed List of Pamphlets on Prostitution forming a special case in the Cleveland Public Library, Mr. Walton acknowledges "a choice selection of pamphlets bearing on the failure of the C.D. Acts in Great Britain, received from the Moral Reform Union."

Berlin.—We were glad to hear that our member, Mrs. Fischer-Lette, had become Honorary Secretary of a Woman's Moral Reform Society in the German capital.

Prague.—Works on Repeal were sent to the President of the Y.M.C.A. here, Miss Taylor contributing three most important German works and "Le Droit de la Femme"; of which Mrs. Louis Blacker sent the German translation also.

Stuttgart.—One of our oldest members having visited this town, wrote to us for introductions. We sent her various German periodicals and also the S.P.A. work, "Purity—Man's Honour," written by the Rev. C. Weitbrecht, the German Pastor at Stuttgart.

Literature.—Our sale to March 31st, 1895, is 1,129 works, value £12 18s. 6d.. Free distribution *from our own stock* was 910 works, value £6 16s. 9d., cost of postage being 17/7¾. Of 12,392 leaflets and works presented to us for free distribution, value £12 1*s.* 10½*d.*—5,495 (value £11 3*s.* 8¼*d.*) have been sent out, postage costing £1 12*s.* 10*d.*

Obituary.—With deep regret we note the loss of Mrs. Stephenson Hunter, of Oxford, and of Mr. Thomas James, of Harrismith, Orange Free States. Nor can we pass in silence the death of one not a member of our Union:—the octogenarian author of "Le Droit de la Femme," Mons. Charles Secrétan, who was during his long life so firm a friend to the cause of woman's progress.

Membership.—We number to-day 150 members, of whom 23 live out of England, and 60 reside at a distance from town.

The Honorary Treasurership.—To our sincere regret, our Hon. Treasurer, Mrs. Miers, after six years' tenure of that onerous post, has felt obliged, for reasons of health, to retire at Midsummer. The loss of a Treasurer combining such excellent qualities of method, exactitude, economy, and generosity, leaves the Society a very difficult task to find a successor to her. Our heart-felt thanks are but inadequate to express our sense of her value.

The Honorary Secretaryship.—From November, 1890, we have had the privilege of having as Hon. Secretary, Miss Helen Taylor. The prestige of her name and character gave an impetus to the Moral

Reform Union on the retirement of its Foundress and first Hon. Secretary, Mrs. Woolcott Browne. We had the ready help of Miss Taylor's ability and intellectual force, her valuable advice, and steady financial support. In the supply, reprinting and dissemination of literature, she was an unwearied friend to the Society and its extension. It may be supposed, therefore, with what disappointment her recent resignation was received on May 1st. On that occasion a resolution was passed embodying our gratitude to Miss Taylor for her valuable help in the past; and it is felt that those present at this our Thirteenth Annual Meeting, will ratify and accentuate that expression of our sense of what we owe so largely to the generosity of our late Honorary Secretary.

At a time when the Press is daily revealing frightful cases of immorality resulting in murder and outrage and the breaking up of homes, we cannot but feel more than ever the need which exists to reach down to and eradicate, by Moral Education, the roots of those evils which are fast sapping the purity of our English home life. As these evils come more and more to the surface of society shocking every moral sense, we need to meet them with moral courage, and, as we said last year, check them by vigilance, earnestness, prudence, and perseverance.

MORAL REFORM UNION.

ANNUAL MEETING,

1895.

The Thirteenth Annual Meeting took place on Wednesday, May 29th, at 3 p.m., by the kind invitation of Mrs. Miers, at 74, Addison Road, Kensington. The Report and Balance Sheet were accepted, and the three following Resolutions adopted :—

(I.) "That since the Society has the same unique position as "when instituted by its Foundress, Mrs. Woolcott "Browne, in April, 1881, the Members and Sub-"scribers present feel perfect confidence in its aim "and motto, and pledge themselves to support both."

(II.) "That this Thirteenth Annual Meeting of the Moral Reform "Union is much moved by the announcement of Miss "Taylor's resignation of the Honorary Secretaryship, "which she has held since November, 1890, and takes "this public opportunity of acknowledging the in-"debtedness of the Union for her able guidance, "which, with her valuable qualities, is testified to in "the Report now laid before this Meeting, and here-"by tenders to her its sincere and warmest thanks."

(III.) "That this Thirteenth Annual Meeting of the Moral "Reform Union, warmly appreciates the sustained "efforts and personal sacrifices which Mrs. Miers "has so continuously made in carrying on the Hono-"rary Treasurership with so much method, exactitude, "and economy, and in enabling it to discharge "its obligations ; and this Meeting hereby offers her "its sincerest thanks and cordial acknowledgments "for her devotion."

SUBSCRIPTIONS AND DONATIONS.

APRIL 1st, 1894, to MARCH 31st, 1895.

	Subs. £ s. d.	Dons. £ s. d.
"A. D. A."	0 5 0	
A Friend (per Miss Stammwitz)		0 3 0
A Christmas Gift		2 0 0
A Friend		5 16 8
A Friend	0 5 0	
A Friend		6 5 3
A Donation for Literature		0 6 0
A. K.	0 10 6	
Browne, Mrs. Woolcott	5 0 0	
Burt, Mrs. C. Johnstone	0 5 0	
Blackwell, Dr. Elizabeth	0 10 0	
Bussell, Miss Ada G.	0 2 6	
Bennett, Miss E.	1 1 0	
Buss, Mrs. Septimus	0 2 6	
Burt, C. W., Esq.	1 1 0	
Brandreth, H. S., Esq.	1 0 0	
Blacker, Mrs. Louis	1 1 0	
Cobb, Mrs. H. P.	0 5 0	
Charles, Mrs.	0 10 0	
Cock, Mrs. Astley	0 5 0	
Carslake, Mrs. Hawkey	1 1 0	
Coles, Mrs....		0 10 6
Conybeare, Miss Emily	0 2 6	
Drew, Mrs....	0 2 6	
Evans, Mrs.	0 4 0	
Eccles, Mr. and Mrs.	2 2 0	
Estlin, Miss M. A.	0 10 6	
E. L. M.		3 0 0
Goff, Miss A.	0 5 0	
Geddes, Mrs.	0 10 0	
Hunter, the late Mrs. Stephenson...	1 1 0	
Hill, Miss Sarah	0 5 0	
Hindley, Mrs.	0 10 0	
Hall, Miss	0 2 6	
Hanson, Thos. Anderson, Esq. (1894)	0 5 0	
" " " " (1895)	0 5 0	
Horsley, H., Esq.	0 5 0	
Hodgson, Mrs.	0 2 6	
Hill, Miss Emily	0 5 0	
Johnson, Miss Agnes	0 2 6	
Jones, Rev. E. Ceredig	0 2 6	
J. S. M. (1894)	0 2 6	
" (1895)	0 5 0	
James, Mrs. Thomas	1 0 0	
Kay Shuttleworth, Miss J.	0 5 0	

	Subs. £ s. d.	Dons. £ s. d.
Lord, Miss Francis (2 years)	0 5 0	
Leach, Mrs. (1894 and 1895)	0 10 0	
Miers, Mrs.	2 0 0	
Martineau, Dr.	1 1 0	
Munroe, Mrs.	0 2 6	
Mitcheson, Rev. T.	0 2 6	
Müller, Mrs.	1 1 0	
Mordan, Miss C. E.	0 2 6	
Malleson, W. T., Esq.	0 2 6	
Meredith, Rev. W. M.	0 5 0	
Newman, Professor Francis	2 0 0	
Naoroji, D. G., Esq., M.P.	0 10 6	
Owen, Rev. J. A. (2 years)	0 10 0	
Payne, Mrs. (2 years)...	0 10 0	
Parnell, Miss Mary	0 5 0	
Phillips, Mrs.	0 5 0	
Pallandt, Baroness de	0 5 0	
Peppercorn, Miss	0 5 0	
Peckover, Miss P. H.	1 0 0	
Reed, Mrs. E.	0 5 0	
Raper, —., Esq.		0 5 0
Smith, Mrs. Pearsall	0 5 0	
Southey, Mrs.	0 5 0	
Stammwitz, Miss Louisa	0 5 0	
Swanwick, Miss	1 1 0	
Strickland, Mrs. F.	0 2 6	
Stansfeld, The Rt. Hon. and Mrs. (1894 and 1895)	0 10 0	
Sherrard, J. C., Esq., J.P.	0 2 6	
Solly, Rev. Henry	0 2 6	
Turner, Mrs.	0 2 6	
Tremenheere, Mrs.	2 0 0	1 0 0
Taylor, Miss Helen (Withdrawn.) ...	20 0 0	30 7 6
Tebb, Mrs. W.	1 1 0	
Tubbs, Mrs.	0 10 6	
Thompson, Francis, Esq.	0 10 0	
Tolmé (paid 1894 in advance)		
Toller, Mrs.	1 1 0	
Thomas, Mrs. C.	1 1 0	
Tucker, Mrs.	0 10 0	
Timmins, Rev. T.	0 2 6	
Walker, Miss E. Abney	0 5 0	
Whale, Mrs. E.	0 5 0	
Wells, Mrs. T. H.	0 5 0	
Weiss, Mrs. Caroline	0 5 0	
Whitehead, Miss C. M.	0 5 0	
Wates, J., Esq.	1 1 0	
Wates, Mrs.	0 10 6	
Wilkinson, Miss (1894 and 1895)	0 15 0	
Wilson, Mr. and Mrs. H. J.	1 0 0	
Watt, D. A., Esq.	0 10 0	
	£68 0 6	£49 13 11

The following are also Members:—

Albert, Miss F. E.
Ashford, Mrs., (P.L.G.)
Askey, Mr. and Mrs. F. D.
Balgarnie, Miss F.
Banks, F. C., Esq.
Barbosa, Mrs. Garnet
Bazett, H., Esq.
Bear, Miss A.
Berdoe, Edward, Esq., M.D.
Bradley, Mrs.
Brodribb, Miss F. H.
Buckle, Miss
Bullen, Rev. Ashington, B.A.
Burd, A. A., Esq.
Burnett, Miss M.
Campbell, Mrs. A. M.
Chant, Mrs. Ormiston
Chapman, Miss E. R.
Clelland, Mrs.
Clifford, Rev. J., D.D., and Mrs.
Cozens, Miss
Dymond, Mrs. Geo.
Ford, Miss I. O.
Fischer-Lette, Mrs.
Geddes, Rev. J. B.
Gilder, Dhanjibhai Dorabji, Esq.
Hack, Mrs. Brocklehurst
Haines, Mrs.
Hammond, Eric, Esq.
Herbert, Jesse, Esq.
Hessë, Emil, Esq.
Hime, C. Maurice, Esq., M.A., LL.D.
Hoggan, Mrs. F. M., M.D.
Kidd, Mrs. Benjamin
Kilgour, Miss
Kirby, The Rev. J. C.
Knight, A. A., Esq.
Law, Mrs. W.
Lodge, L., Esq.
Löfving, Miss Concordia
Magnüsson, Mrs.
Malleson, W. T., Esq.
Mason, Miss
McLaren, J. S., Esq., M.D.
Meredith, Mrs.
Meredith, Mrs. W. M.
Mills, H. L., Esq.
Minet, Miss G.
Misra, U. S., Esq., B.U.C.S.
Mitchell, Mrs. C. T.
Mitcheson, Mrs.
Müller, Miss
Nathan, Mrs. H.
Ockenden, James, Esq.
Paggi, Madame
Pease, T. H. O., Esq.
Rossell-Jones, Mrs.
Rudge, Miss
Sherrard, Mrs.
Shuttleworth, Miss J. Kay
Steinthal, The Rev. A. S.
Steward, Mrs.
Storr, F., Esq.
Streatfeild, Mr. and Mrs. W. H.
Teshmacher, Mrs.
Thomas, Mrs. E.
Thomas, Miss R.
Tod, Miss I.
Tournier, Miss E. A.
Trepplin, Mrs.
Varley, Mrs. H.
Venning, Miss
Walters, Mrs.
Wild, Mademoiselle
Williams, A., Esq.
Williams, Mrs. Howard
Williams, Rev. H.
Williams, Miss J.

THE MORAL REFORM UNION.

Statements of Receipts and Expenditure, for the year ending 31st March, 1895.

Receipts.

	£	s.	d.
To Balance from last year (31st March, 1894)	17	1	3
,, Subscriptions	68	0	6
,, Donations	49	13	11
,, Donations to "*Coote Memorial*"	35	8	6
,, Sale of Literature	12	18	6
	£183	2	8

Expenditure.

	£	s.	d.	£	s.	d.
By Rent of Office				35	0	0
,, Literature				5	5	4
,, Stationery and Sundries				2	2	1
,, Secretary's Salary				70	0	0
,, Printing				6	8	6
,, Postage				7	10	8
,, Firing, Lighting, Office Expenses, and Caretaker, etc.				19	7	5
,, "Coote Memorial"				35	8	6
				£181	2	6
,, Balance at Bank ...	£0	3	9			
,, Cash in hand ...	1	16	5			
				2	0	2
				£183	2	8

Examined, compared with the Books and Vouchers, and found correct,

M. Harris Smith, *Auditor.*
(public accountant.)

13, Victoria Street, Westminster, S.W., and
Royal Bank Buildings,
123, Bishopsgate Street Within, E.C.

6th April, 1895.

www.ingramcontent.com/pod-product-compliance
Lightning Source LLC
LaVergne TN
LVHW080020110826
845148LV00019B/1174

* 9 7 8 1 5 3 5 8 1 3 5 9 4 *